*With special thanks*
*To Martin Kerr for beautiful book design.*
*To Helen Exley for believing in my work and your constant wise*
*counsel throughout this project.*
*To my husband Jim, for everything.*
*Dedication: To my son, Brent*

Published in 2004 by Exley Publications Ltd in Great Britain.
16 Chalk Hill, Watford, Herts WD19 4BG, UK

Published in 2004 by Exley Publications LLC in the USA.
185 Main Street, Spencer, MA 01562, USA

www.helenexleygiftbooks.com

12 11 10 9 8 7 6 5 4 3 2 1

Copyright © Susan Squellati Florence 2004.

The moral right of the author has been asserted.

ISBN 1-86187-724-2

Edited by Helen Exley. Printed in China.

Written and illustrated by Susan Squellati Florence
www.susanflorence.com

*Helen Exley Giftbooks cover the most powerful of all human*
*relationships: love between couples, the bonds within families and*
*between friends. No expense is spared in making sure that each book*
*is as thoughtful and meaningful a gift as it is possible to create: good*
*to give, good to receive. You have the result in your hands. If you*
*have loved it — tell others! We'd rather put the money into more good*
*books than spend it on advertising. There is no power on earth like*
*the word-of-mouth recommendation of friends.*

# THE GIFT
# OF NOW

*...the simple joy of just being*

WRITTEN & ILLUSTRATED BY

## Susan Squellati Florence

A HELEN EXLEY GIFTBOOK

*We* are all in a hurry going nowhere. And before we even get there... we are moving on to somewhere else. We are working hard for what we want... and we always want more. We start things and then before we are finished, begin something new. Everyday we do things without thinking about them... because we are lost in busy thoughts. I can say all of this from my own experience.

This book is a reminder for us all to pause in the rush through today and see what is right there before us... to stop and be a part of the moment. When we are rethinking yesterday and planning tomorrow... we miss out on what is happening right now.

When we tune into the moment and try to live deliberately... something happens. It may be that you will be able to really listen to the person who is talking to you. It may be that you will look up and notice the beauty of green leaves shimmering in sunlight. It may be that you will notice your own breath. Whatever it is... you will feel more connected to yourself, to others and to everything that surrounds you.

The world will continue to pull you into its fast moving spin. I hope this book can help to bring you back to the moments of your day and the joy and satisfaction of "being" in the gift of now.

*The gift of now may come to you*
*in an instant of awareness*
*or gradually*
*through the years.*

*The gift of now*
*may come because something*
*is changing inside you.*
*You are seeing life*
*with new eyes.*

*The gift of now*
*may come to you,*
*like it did to me,*
*when I was alive with ideas*
*of everything I wanted to do...*

*when my mind was so completely full*
*of lists and plans and dreams*
*of things to do...*
*that I knew*
*they would not happen.*

And then
I had a strange insight...
that doing all these things
might not matter.
I realized
that there was something more
than everything I wanted to do.

*There is something
enormous and extraordinary
already happening in my life
and it is always happening...*

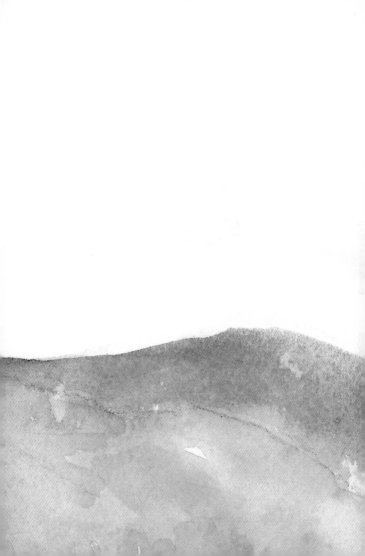

*...it is this moment...*

*it is now.*

I had been driving for hours
completely lost in thought.
I looked around at
hillsides and purple wildflowers
growing everywhere
and realized I had not seen
the beauty surrounding me.

*I was missing out on what was there*
*right before my eyes.*

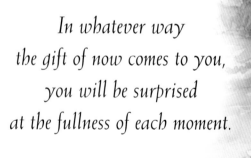

*In whatever way*
*the gift of now comes to you,*
*you will be surprised*
*at the fullness of each moment.*

*This special gift*
*of just being*
*may come as you work at your desk.*
*You might catch yourself*
*mindlessly racing*
*through what you are doing.*
*You may stop and just sit.*
*You may slow down*
*and notice the rhythm*
*of your own deep breathing.*

The simple gift of being
may surprise you
while you are preparing your salad
You may look down
and become aware
of what you are doing.
You may begin to really see
the crispy lettuce
and marvel
at the red of the tomato.

*There is a joy
of being
in the moment.*

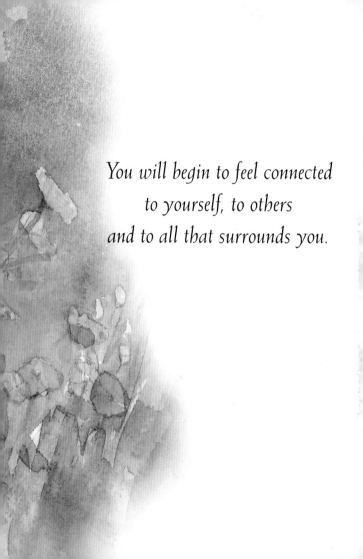

*You will begin to feel connected
to yourself, to others
and to all that surrounds you.*

You will be able to stay with yourself
and let life pass through you,
instead of passing through life
in a hurry.

*Being alive in the moment*
*without doing everything else*
*is wonderful.*
*Being alive in the moment*
*without doing anything else*
*is sublime.*

*Every moment
is sacred.*

*Take time to pause*
*and feel the golden gift of life.*

*Take time to really listen
to each other.
Take time to forgive,
time to forget.*

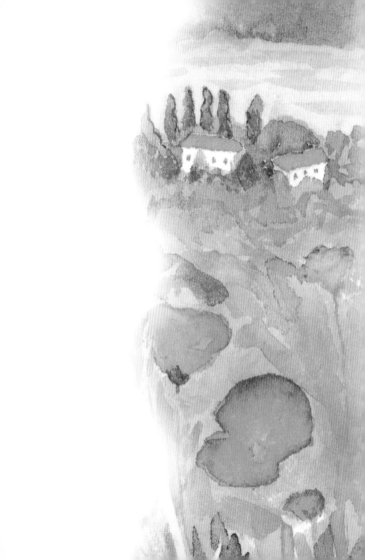

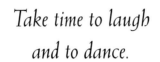

*Take time to laugh
and to dance.*

*Yesterday is always with us*
*and yesterday*
*is always gone.*
*Tomorrow is not yet born...*
*and we cannot hold it.*

*Today is real.*
*It is completely full*
*like a fruit when it's ripe,*
*like a benevolent rose*
*open to the sun,*
*to the rain,*
*giving of itself entirely.*

*You can make your life
what you want it to be.*

You can give yourself entirely
to this moment
and receive everything
this moment brings.

*You can be a part*
*of all that surrounds you*
*and be connected to*
*the people who are with you.*

*You can*
*just be.*

Open the gift of now.
Look inside and see.

It is you
it is life
it is precious.

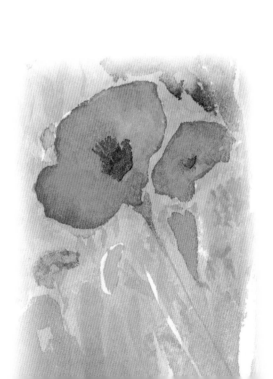

# THE JOURNEYS SERIES

1-86187-420-0

## Change...
*is a place where new journeys begin*

1-86187-422-7

*How wonderful it is...*

## Having Friends in Our Lives

1-86187-729-3

## Let Happiness Be Yours
*...a wish for life's greatest gift*

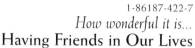

1-86187-418-9

## On the Gift of A Mother's Love
*For my mother from your daughter
a mother too*

1-86187-419-7

## Take Time Alone
*The gift of being with yourself*

1-86187-724-2

## The Gift of Now
*...the simple joy of just being*

1-86187-421-9

## When You Lose Someone You Love
*...a journey through the heart of grief*

1-86187-417-0

## Your Journey
*...a passage through a difficult time*

# ABOUT THE AUTHOR

*The well loved and collected greeting cards of Susan Florence have sold hundreds of millions of copies in the last three decades. Her giftbooks have sold over one and a half million copies.*

*With gentle words and original paintings, Susan Florence brings her unique style to all of her gift products and her readers have written time and again to thank her for the profound help her books have been to them. People have said that her words speak to them of what they cannot say... but what they feel.*

*Susan has created a completely new line of giftbooks called The Journeys Series. With soft, free paintings and simple, sincere words, the Journeys books are gifts of connection, comfort, and inspiration to give those special to us.*

*As one reader wrote: "Susan Florence's wise and beautiful books have a quiet, healing power about them. What a gift she offers in encouraging us to slow down and deepen our connection to ourselves, our transitions and our closest relationships."*

*Susan lives with her husband, Jim, in Ojai, California. They have two grown children, Brent and Emily.*